A Time to Love

Helen Steiner Rice

A Time to Love

HUTCHINSON
London Melbourne Auckland Johannesburg

The prayers in this volume are taken from The Book of Common Prayer of the Protestant Episcopal Church. The Church Hymnal Corporation and the Seabury Press, 1979.

Scripture quotations in this book are taken from The Holy Bible: New International Version. Copyright © 1973, 1978 by the International Bible Society. Used by permission of Zondervan Bible Publishers.

Special thanks to Virginia J. Ruehlmann of the Helen Steiner Rice Foundation for her assistance in researching materials.

First published in Great Britain in 1987 by Hutchinson Ltd, an imprint of
Century Hutchinson Ltd, Brookmount House, 62–65 Chandos Place, London WC2N 4NW

Century Hutchinson Australia Pty Ltd
PO Box 496, 16–22 Church Street, Hawthorn, Victoria 3122, Australia

Century Hutchinson New Zealand Limited
PO Box 40–086, Glenfield, Auckland 10, New Zealand

Century Hutchinson South Africa (Pty) Ltd
PO Box 337, Bergvlei, 2012 South Africa

ISBN   0 09 172623 9

British Library Cataloguing in Publication Data

Rice, Helen Steiner
  A time to love.
  I. Title
  811' .54   PS3568.I28
ISBN 0-09-172623-9

Set in Bembo by Book Ens, Saffron Walden, Essex
Printed and bound in Great Britain by (to supply)

Contents

*There is a time for everything, and a
season for every activity under heaven.*   *Ecclesiastes 3:1*

A Part of Me

Dear God, You are a part of me
You're all I hear and all I see
You're what I say and what I do
For all my life belongs to You
You walk with me and talk with me
For I am Yours eternally
And when I stumble, slip, and fall
Because I'm weak and lost and small
You help me up and take my hand
And lead me toward the Promised Land
I cannot dwell apart from You,
You would not ask or want me to,
For You have room within Your heart
To make each child of Yours a part
Of You and all Your love and care

Publisher's Foreword

There is a time for everything,
       and a season for every activity under heaven:
a time to be born and a time to die,
a time to plant and a time to uproot,
a time to kill and a time to heal,
a time to tear down and a time to build,
a time to weep and a time to laugh,
a time to mourn and a time to dance,
a time to scatter stones and a time to gather them,
a time to embrace and a time to refrain,
a time to search and a time to give up,
a time to keep and a time to throw away,
a time to tear and a time to mend,
a time to be silent and a time to speak,
a time to love and a time to hate,
a time for war and a time for peace.
Ecclesiastes 3:1–8 NIV

    The poet who penned these lines captured in their simplest form life's fundamental truths. The words seem common, the thoughts obvious. But in reading, we discover a curious comfort in these simple words, whose very cadence echoes the deepest rhythms of our lives.

    Our lives are measured by rhythms. The first months of life are marked by the beat of our mother's heart. God patterns our lives with the ebb and flow of the ocean tides, the phases of the moon, and the turning of the seasons. The festivals and fastings of the church year mark our spiritual seasons. And each one of us has her own personal, unique set of celebrations and remembrances: the birthday of a friend, the death of a spouse, the anniversary of a marriage. Indeed, it would be impossible to imagine our lives without these rhythms. Through them, we are able to savour the past, embrace the present, and reach for the future.

Poets are especially attuned to these rhythms of life, and Helen Steiner Rice was no exception. Helen totally embraced life and its many changes; she personally experienced its ebb and flow. She knew exhilarating joy and heartbreaking sorrow. She understood the butterfly-in-the-tummy happiness of a new love and the sad loss of a beloved husband. In short she embraced in grand fashion the celebrations of life. She used these seasons and rhythms to restore order, to encourage the wounded, to comfort the mourning, to rejoice with the newlyweds, to celebrate a new arrival, to reflect on the simple, good things in life.

Her poems were written to commemorate events. She often sent specially composed poems—congratulations to a niece who was getting married, expressions of joy to a co-worker who just had a child, a letter offering solace to a grieving friend.

We have gathered her poems and letters marking the rhythms of life under lines from Ecclesiastes, adding as seasoning passages from Scripture and traditional prayers. Our intention is to allow you the reader to experience the comfort and joy in the seasons of life that Helen wished for each of her many readers. You may wish to start at the beginning and relish the patterns and pace of the book as a whole, or you may prefer to pick out a section of poems that will meet a specific need in your life. However you chose to read her work, we encourage you to open yourself to that gift of hope that Helen offered to all her readers.

Go with joy.

A Time to Be Born

And Mary said:

"My soul praises the Lord
    and my spirit rejoices in God my Savior,
for he has been mindful of the humble state of his
    servant.
From now on all generations will call me blessed,
    for the Mighty One has done great things for me—
    holy is his name.
His mercy extends to those who fear him,
    from generation to generation.
He has performed mighty deeds with his arm;
    he has scattered those who are proud in their
    inmost thoughts.
He has brought down rulers from their thrones
    but has lifted up the humble.
He has filled the hungry with good things
    but has sent the rich away empty.
He has helped his servant Israel,
    remembering to be merciful
to Abraham and his descendants forever,
    even as he said to our fathers."

Luke 1:46–55

Tender Words of Welcome for the New Baby

Welcome to this world we live in!
Your coming has been eagerly awaited, and now that you are here, Mommy and Daddy are so proud of you!

You are starting life surrounded by love and affection, for your parents are devoted to you. And in the shelter of their loving arms, your babyhood will be comfortable, safe, and happy! And always your Heavenly Father, who sent you as a Gift of Love to bless your Mommy and Daddy, will have you in His Care so no harm can befall you.

From the moment of your birth, you have embarked on a Great Adventure. You have so many things to learn—things about yourself, about the world, and about the people all around you. You will learn to appreciate Beauty. You will experience the joy of sharing and caring. You will come to know the satisfaction of work well done. You will have sunny days and happy hours, but there will be times when the clouds are heavy and the going is tough, and you will know the pain of dark hours and anxiety and uncertainty. There will be many to help you along the way, and, in turn, you will help others. For in helping others, we are *helping ourselves*, and in kindness to others, we serve and help our Father in heaven, too! You will do your part to make this world a better place in which to live, and God will look down and bless you!

The Little Heartbreaker

Who steals into your heart
With magical touch,
Who ensnares your love
In a wee angel clutch,

Who makes you a slave
And a worshipper, too,
Who gets adoration
So lavish and true,

Who plays with your heartstrings
Like a champion Love-maker?
Nobody but baby
The little heartbreaker.

A Gift of Life

A baby is a gift of life
        born of "the wonder of love,"
A little bit of eternity
        sent from the Father above,
Giving a new dimension
        to the love between husband and wife
And putting an added new meaning
        to the wonder and mystery of life!

What Is a Baby?

A wee bit of heaven
Drifted down from above,
A handful of happiness,
A heart full of love—

Wonder of wonders,
So soft, sweet, and small,
Without which there'd be
Just no life at all!

Greatest Career Is Womanhood

So glad a tiny baby came
To share your life and love and name
For no doubt she is the greatest claim
That you have ever had to fame
And don't misunderstand me, dear
You were a "star" in your career.
But what, I ask you, is success
Compared to "heaven's happiness"
And how could "plaudits" anywhere
Be half as wonderful and fair?
For this experience of the heart
Surpasses any skill or art
And no awards that you may win
Will "thrill you" like wee Laura Lynn
For man excels in every line
But woman has a gift divine
And in this world there is no other
As greatly honored as a mother.

Ten Little Fingers

Ten little fingers
Ten little toes
Tiny as a minute
Sweet as a rose . . .
One of life's mysteries
Which nobody knows . . .
And one of the miracles
Only God can disclose.

Almighty God, heavenly Father,
You have blessed us with the joy and care of children:
Give us calm strength and patient wisdom
as we bring them up, that we may teach them
to love whatever is just and good and true.
Amen.

A Gift From Above

I'm so glad
    your home has been blessed
With the Dearest and Sweetest
    and most sacredly best
Of all of life's gifts
    that come from above
And are born of the beauty
    and wonder of love . . .
For God sends "small angels"
    to a husband and wife
To add deeper meaning
    to their married life . . .

And while she is yours
      to fondle and love,
She really belongs
      to her Father above
And God only entrusted
      "His Angel" to you,
So ask Him for guidance
      in all that you do
And tell her that Jesus
      has her in His care
And, whenever she needs Him,
      He will be there!

A Bundle of Heavenly Joy

Your marriage has been truly blessed
For with your new son's birth
God sent an Angel down from heaven
To live with you on earth
For I think God up in heaven
Looks down on couples in love
And blesses their happy union
With a gift of His love from above
And so through this tiny Angel
He has drawn you together for life,
For now you are father and mother
Instead of just husband and wife
And while he is yours to fondle,
To care for, to teach, and to love,
He belongs to his Father in heaven,
For he came from His home up above
So ask Him for guidance in molding
The future of your little boy,
For he is a "jewel" from His kingdom
Sent to bring you "heavenly joy!"

Thoughts of Love on Your Birthday

Birthdays are occasion
    for compliments and praise
And saying many of the things
    we don't say other days—
For thoughts of love and gratitude
    are fragile, cherished things,
As gossamer as fleecy clouds
    or hummingbirds' small wings,
And often through the passing days
    we feel deep down inside
Unspoken thoughts of thankfulness
    and fond, admiring pride—
But words can say so little
    when the heart is overflowing
And often those we love the most
    must have no way of knowing
The many things the heart conceals
    and never can impart,
For words seem so inadequate
    to express what's in the heart—
But since it is your birthday
    I thought it would be nice
If I let this first edition verse
    by Helen Steiner Rice
In some small way express the things
    that I would like to say
Not only on your birthday
    but on every other day.

Another Birthday
And Another Year Closer
to God!

Your many years of loving God
      have been golden years well spent,
Which have brought a "golden harvest"
      of deep serene content . . .
For glorious is the gladness
      and rich is the reward
Of all who work unceasingly
      in the service of the Lord . . .
And I know our Heavenly Father
      has directd you each day
As you tried to serve and please Him
      as you followed in His way . . .
And looking back across your life
      your spirit grows serene
As your soul in love envisions
      what your eyes have never seen . . .
And while the springtime of your life
      is pleasant to recall,
You know the autumn of life
      is the richest time of all . . .
For great has been your gladness
      and priceless your reward
As through the years you walked with joy
      in "The Vineyard of the Lord,"
For to know God and to serve Him
      is a "Joy beyond all price"—
And no one knows this better
      than Helen Steiner Rice!

A Birthday Blessing

May your birthday be especially blest
With all that makes you happiest
And may He who hears our smallest prayer
Keep you always in His Care.

Birthdays Are a Gift From God

Where does *time* go in its endless flight—
Spring turns to fall and day to night,
And birthdays come and birthdays go
And where they go we do not know . . .
But God who planned our life on earth
And gave our mind and body birth
And then enclosed a living soul
With heaven as the spirit's goal
Has given man the gift of choice
To follow that small inner voice
That speaks to us from year to year
Reminding us we've naught to fear . . .
For *birthdays* are a *stepping-stone*
To endless joys as yet unknown,
So fill each day with happy things
And may your burdens all take wings
And fly away and leave behind
Great joy of heart and peace of mind . . .
For *birthdays* are *the gateway* to
An *endless life of joy for you*
If you but pray from day to day
That He will show you the *Truth* and the *Way*.

Watch over thy child, O Lord, as his days increase;
bless and guide him wherever he may be.
Strengthen him when he stands;
comfort him when discouraged or sorrowful;
raise him up if he falls;
and in his heart may thy peace which passeth understanding
abide all the days of his life.
Amen.

Another Happy Year

The years go by so swiftly
    I simply can't conceive
That tomorrow is your birthday
    and once more you'll receive
Birthday cards that wish you
    another happy year,
But I can't dispute the calendar
    so "Happy Birthday," dear . . .
And while the "way" gets rougher
    as we "climb the rising slope,"
As long as we have courage
    and love and faith and hope,
We can go on undaunted
    in the blessed reassurance
That God will "lift our burdens"
    and give us "new endurance" . . .
And you and I know, my dear friend,
    that God and God alone
Could make it possible to bear
    the "burdens you have known" . . .

And He has brought you safely
  through many troubled hours
And warmed your heart with "sunshine"
    that always followed "showers" . . .
And as you start another year
    here's hoping you will find
Some unexpected happiness
    and abiding peace of mind.

A Time to Love

And now I will show you the most excellent way.

If I speak in the tongues of men and of angels, but have not love, I am only a resounding gong or a clanging cymbal. If I have the gift of prophecy and can fathom all mysteries and all knowledge, and if I have a faith that can move mountains, but have not love, I am nothing. If I give all I possess to the poor and surrender my body to the flames, but have not love, I gain nothing.

Love is patient, love is kind. It does not envy, it does not boast, it is not proud. It is not rude, it is not self-seeking, it is not easily angered, it keeps no record of wrongs. Love does not delight in evil but rejoices with the truth. It always protects, always trusts, always hopes, always perseveres.

Love never fails. But where there are prophecies, they will cease; where there are tongues, they will be stilled; where there is knowledge, it will pass away. For we know in part and we prophesy in part, but when perfection comes, the imperfect disappears. When I was a child, I talked like a child, I thought like a child, I reasoned like a child. When I became a man, I put childish ways behind me. Now we see but a poor reflection; then we shall see face to face. Now I know in part; then I shall know fully, even as I am fully known.

And now these three remain: faith, hope and love. But the greatest of these is love.

1 *Corinthians 12:31–13:13*

He Loves You!

It's amazing and incredible,
But it's as true as it can be,
God loves and understands us all
And that means you and me—
His grace is all sufficient
For both the young and old,
For the lonely and the timid,
For the brash and for the bold—
His love knows no exceptions,
So never feel excluded
No matter who or what you are
Your name has been included—
And no matter what your past has been,
Trust God to understand,
And no matter what your problem is
Just place it in His hand—
For in all of our unloveliness
This great God loves us still,
He loved us since the world began
And what's more, He *always will!*

Love: God's Gift Divine

Love is enduring
And patient and kind,
It judges all things
With the heart not the mind,
And love can transform
The most commonplace
Into beauty and splendor
And sweetness and grace . . .
For love is unselfish,
Giving more than it takes,
And no matter what happens
Love never forsakes,
It's faithful and trusting
And always believing,
Guileless and honest
And never deceiving . . .
Yes, love is beyond
What man can define,
For love is immortal
And God's Gift is Divine!
And underneath this refuge
Are the everlasting arms—
So cast your burden on Him,
Seek His counsel when distressed,
And go to Him for comfort
When you're lonely and oppressed—
For God is our encouragement
In trouble and in trials,
And in suffering and in sorrow
He will turn our tears to smiles.

Where There Is Love

Where there is love the heart is light,
Where there is love the day is bright,
Where there is love there is a song
To help when things are going wrong,
Where there is love there is a smile
To make all things seem more worthwhile,
Where there is love there's quiet peace,
A tranquil place where turmoils cease . . .
Love changes darkness into light
And makes the heart take "wingless flight"—
Oh, blest are they who walk in love . . .
They also walk with God above,
And when man walks with God again
There shall be Peace on Earth for men.

To Meet Old Friends

Somehow, meeting old friends
and embracing them with your heart
is like the "warmth of a home fireside"
and the "loveliness of a rose garden."
All the vexations and irritations of a busy day
were softened by the remembrance
of that "shining hour"
we spent together this morning.

What More Can You Ask

God's love endureth forever—
What a wonderful thing to know
When the tides of life run against you
And your spirit is downcast and low . . .
God's kindness is ever around you,
Always ready to freely impart
Strength to your faltering spirit,
Cheer to your lonely heart . . .
God's presence is ever beside you,
As near as the reach of your hand,
You have but to tell Him your troubles,
There is nothing He won't understand . . .
And knowing God's love is unfailing,
And His mercy unending and great,
You have but to trust in His promise—
"God comes not too soon or too late" . . .
So wait with a heart that is patient
For the goodness of God to prevail—
For never do prayers go unanswered,
And His mercy and love never fail.

The Gift of Friendship

Friendship is a priceless gift
That cannot be bought or sold,
But its value is far greater
Than a mountain made of gold—
For gold is cold and lifeless,
It can neither see nor hear,
And in the time of trouble
It is powerless to cheer—
It has no ears to listen,
No heart to understand,
It cannot bring you comfort
Or reach out a helping hand—
So when you ask God for a Gift,
Be thankful if He sends
Not diamonds, pearls, or riches,
But the love of real true friends.

The Magic of Love

Love is like Magic
And it always will be,
For love still remains
Life's sweet mystery!

Love works in ways
That are wondrous and strange
And there's nothing in life
That love cannot change!

Love can transform
The most commonplace
Into beauty and splendor
And sweetness and grace!

Love is unselfish,
Understanding and kind,
For it sees with its heart
And not with its mind!

Love is the answer
That everyone seeks—
Love is the language
That every heart speaks—

Love can't be bought,
It is priceless and free,
Love like pure magic
Is a sweet mystery!

Romance

If you have Romance don't sell it—
Keep it—treasure it—cherish it
It is worth all odds
For while you have romance, you have love
But once you mistreat it,
It will leave you
And then you are poor indeed
For you have lost love.

Listen! My lover!
  Look! Here he comes,
leaping across the mountains,
  bounding over the hills.
My lover is like a gazelle or a young stag.
  Look! There he stands behind our wall,
gazing through the windows,
  peering through the lattice.
My lover spoke and said to me,
  "Arise, my darling,
  my beautiful one, and come with me.
See! The winter is past;
  the rains are over and gone.
Flowers appear on the earth;
  the season of singing has come,
the cooing of doves
  is heard in our land.
The fig tree forms its early fruit;
  the blossoming vines spread their fragrance.
Arise, come, my darling;
  my beautiful one, come with me."

Song of Songs 2:8–13

The Gift of Lasting Love

Love is much more than a tender caress
  and more than bright hours of gay happiness,
For a lasting love is made up of sharing
  both hours that are "joyous" and also
  "despairing" . . .

It's made up of patience and deep understanding
      and never of selfish and stubborn demanding,
It's made up of climbing the steep hills together
      and facing with courage life's stormiest weather
And nothing on earth or in heaven can part
      a love that has grown to be part of the heart,
And just like the sun and the stars and the sea,
      this love will go on through *eternity*—
For "true love" lives on when earthly things die,
      for it's part of the Spirit that soars to the sky.

The Meaning of True Love

It is sharing and caring,
Giving and forgiving,
Loving and being loved,
Walking hand in hand,
Talking heart to heart,
Seeing through each other's eyes,
Laughing together,
Weeping together,
Praying together,
And always trusting
And believing
And thanking God
For each other . . .
For love that is shared
      is a beautiful thing—
It enriches the soul
      and makes the heart sing!

If I Could Tell You

It's such a quiet lovely thing
It doesn't ask for much
It isn't untamed longing
That cries for passion's touch
It's not built upon the "quicksand"
Of a pair of lips and arms
For only "false foundations"
Are raised on physical charms
I wish that I could tell you
About this thing I feel
It's intangible like gossamer
But like a hoop of steel
It binds me very close to you
And opens up the door
To more real deep contentment
Than I've ever known before
You see your music reaches
Beyond where words dare pass
It's like a "soul's communion"
Or a sacred Holy Mass
It's something indefinable
Like sea and sky and sod
It might be just enchantment
But I like to think it's God.

Remember These Words

We are gathered together
on this happy day
To stand before God

and to reverently say:
I take thee to be
      my partner for life,
To love and to live with
      as husband and wife;
To have and to hold
      forever, sweetheart,
Through sickness and health
      until death do us part;
To love and to cherish
      whatever betide,
And in better or worse
      to stand by your side
We do this not lightly
      but solemnly, Lord,
Asking Thy blessing
      as we live in accord
With Thy Holy Precepts
      which join us in love
And assure us Thy guidance
      and grace from above
And grant us, dear Lord,
      that "I will" and "I do"
Are words that grow deeper
      and more meaningful, too,
Through long happy years
      of caring and sharing,
Secure in the knowledge
      that we are preparing
A love that is endless
      and never can die
But finds its fulfillment
      with You in the "sky."

A Marriage Blessing

As you enter into the little world
that you promised to make brighter for each other,
may He who harnesses the waves
and hangs the sun out in the sky
and puts the song in the birds
especially bless you
and make your marriage a good and a happy one!

Love is indeed "a many splendored thing!"
When it is given and returned,
it enriches both the Lover and the Beloved.
And as long as two people love each other,
nothing in this world is too difficult or too impossible,
for wanting to do something for the one you love
takes all the burden out of it
and the roughest way becomes smooth
when you can travel it hand in hand.

On Your Wedding Day

I know your heart is filled with a happiness that is so breathtakingly wonderful that it makes you almost afraid! You wish you could capture and hold this beautiful joy forever changeless and unchanging through the years, but, great shining hours, like your wedding day, cannot continue at this pinnacle of ecstasy or your heart would surely burst with the beauty of it.

But God is Love and He made the human heart capable of this great miracle of love so that we might glimpse heaven and experience that divine touch, and in the wonder and awe of this newfound glory we might feel His nearness and realize that it is He and He alone who can make love eternal.

So, I ask that God grant you *faith in each other* and *faith in Him* so that your love becomes part of His love, and with His guidance and His blessing, may you live together bravely and beautifully, sharing sunshine and rain . . . smiles and tears . . . bitter and sweet! May your faith in God and each other give you the strength and the patience to overcome the temptations of impulsive young hearts, so that no misunderstandings may divide you or disturb you. Through the years, may your physical love become a "GREAT LIGHT" that illuminates the soul so that the "tranquil loveliness of eventide" is even more wonderful than the "glory of love's dawn."

May God bless your Wedding Day, hallow your marriage night, and sanctify your motherhood if He sees fit to grant you that privilege.

Today you love each other with your hearts . . . but with God's eye upon you, you will come to love each other with your souls and then, my dear, *your love is eternal*, and *you will take it with you to the skies.*

To Franklin

In my eyes there lies no vision
But the sight of your dear face
In my heart there is no feeling
But the warmth of your embrace
In my mind there are no thoughts
But the thoughts of you, my dear
In my soul no other longing
But just to have you near
All my dreams are built around you
And I've come to know it's true
In my life there is no living
That is not a part of you.

The Joys of Remembering

There's a heap of satisfaction
To sit here thinking of you,
And to tell you once again, dear,
How very much I love you,
There is comfort just in longing
For a smile from your dear face
And joy in just remembering
Each sweet and fond embrace,
There is happiness in knowing
That my heart will always be
A place where I can hold you
And keep you near to me.

An Anniversary Blessing

You've come a long way,
    over smooth roads and rough,
But you've had each other
    and that was enough,
For even the darkest
    and stormiest weather
Brings a "rainbow of love"
    when you share it together
And because you have shared
    your smiles and your tears,
You've built up "rich treasures"
    in these many years
For the memories of things
    you've both shared and faced
Are engraved in your hearts
    and they can't be erased,
And life with its problems
    has been but the blending
Of a love that's divine
    and therefore unending
For love that endures
    through a long, earthly life
And keeps folks together
    as husband and wife
Is fashioned by God
    and you both have been true
To the marriage vows
    that were taken by you . . .
And all of your children
    and their children, too,
And their children's children
    are so proud of you,
For you are a couple
    who walked with the Lord

And a long, fruitful life
    is the good Lord's reward . . .
So here's to the groom
    and here's to the bride
Who for many long years
    have stood side by side!

A Time to Heal

*He who dwells in the shelter of the Most High
    will rest in the shadow of the Almighty.
I will say of the LORD, "He is my refuge and my fortress,
    my God in whom I trust."*

*Surely he will save you from the fowler's snare
    and from the deadly pestilence.
He will cover you with his feathers,
    and under his wings you will find refuge;
    his faithfulness will be your shield and rampart.
You will not fear the terror of night,
    nor the arrow that flies by day,
nor the pestilence that stalks in the darkness,
    nor the plague that destroys at midday.
A thousand my fall at your side,
    ten thousand at your right hand,
    but it will not come near you.
You will only observe with your eyes.
    and see the punishment of the wicked.*

If you make the Most High your dwelling—
even the LORD, who is my refuge—
then no harm will befall you,
no disaster will come near your tent.
For he will command his angels concerning you
to guard you in all your ways;
they will lift you up in their hands,
so that you will not strike your foot against a
stone.
You will tread upon the lion and the cobra;
you will trample the great lion and the serpent.

"Because he loves me," says the LORD, "I will rescue
him;
I will protect him, for he acknowledges my
name.
He will call upon me, and I will answer him;
I will be with him in trouble,
I will deliver him and honor him.
With long life will I satisfy him
and show him my salvation."

Psalm 91

A Seed Is Sown

Seed must be sown to
Bring forth the grain,
And nothing is born
Without suffering and pain
And God never ploughs in
The soul of man
Without intention and
Purpose and plan.

A Special Prayer for You

Oh, Blessed Father, hear this prayer
    and keep all of us in Your care
Give us patience and inner sight, too,
    just as You often used to do
When on the shores of the Galilee
    You touched the blind and they could see
And cured the man who long was lame
    when he but called Your Holy Name!

You are so Great
    we are so small
And when trouble comes
    as it does to us all
There's so little that we can do
    except to place our trust in You!
So take the Saviour's loving Hand
    and do not try to understand
Just let Him lead you where He will
    through "pastures green and waters still"
And place yourself in His loving care
    and He will gladly help you bear
Whatever lies ahead of you
    and God will see you safely through
And no earthly pain is ever too much
    if God bestows His merciful touch.

So I commend you into His care
    with a loving thought and a Special Prayer
And always remember, Whatever betide you
    God is always beside you
And you cannot go beyond His love and care
    for we are all a part of God,
    and God is everywhere!

Comfort in Illness

It makes me sad to think of you
Filled with pain and discomfort, too
But I know there's nothing I can do
But talk to the Lord and pray for you

I wish I could wipe away every trace
Of pain and suffering from your face
But HE is *great* and we are small
We just can't alter His will at all

And none of us would want to try
For more and more, as days go by,
We know His plan for us is best
And He will give us Peace and Rest

And earthly pain is never too much
If He has bestowed His merciful touch
And if you look to Him and Pray
He will help you through every day.

A Prayer for Patience and Comfort

So, realizing my helplessness
    I'm asking God if He will bless
The thoughts you think and all you do
    So these "dark hours" you're passing through
Will lose their grave anxiety
    And only deep tranquillity
Will fill your mind and help impart
    New strength and courage to your heart
So, take the Saviour's loving hand
    And do not try to understand
Just let Him lead you where He will
    Through "pastures green" and "waters still" . . .
And though the way ahead seems steep
    Be not afraid, for He will keep
Tender watch through night and day
    And He will hear each prayer you pray
So, place yourself in His loving care
    And He will gladly help you bear
Whatever lies ahead of you
    For there is nothing God can't do . . .

For God is your Father and you are His own!

So, I commend you into God's care
    And each day I will say a prayer
That you will feel His presence near
    To help dissolve your every fear!

A Garden of Sunshine

Just peeping in to say hello
    and wish you well, my dear
If I could "hang the sunshine out"
    you'd never shed a tear
But life is meant for teardrops
    and loneliness and sorrow
But God has promised *sunshine*
    in *the garden of tomorrow!*
And He will bless and keep you
    in His tender care
For we are all a part of God
    and God is *everywhere.*

All Things Pass

Let all your thoughts be happy, dear,
To chase away all thoughts of fear.
Think of lovely things you've seen
Like rolling slopes of velvet green,
Fluffy clouds of azure blue,
Sparkling drops of crystal dew
Robin redbreasts on the wing
Telling us again it's spring,
Golden beds of daffodils,
Violets blooming on a hill . . .
Don't "cloud" your mind with anxious fear,
Just fill your heart with "sunny cheer,"
And waiting days will soon be over
And you'll again be "back in clover"
For "*all things pass*" . . . and this will, too,
And with God's help you'll come "smiling through."

A Prayer for Healing

I just wish I knew some magic words to say
To take your troubles all away,
But at times like these we realize
That God who is both kind and wise,
Can do what none of us can do
And that's to *heal* and comfort you
So I commend you to His care
And may He hear your smallest prayer
And grant returning health to you
As only He alone can do.

Into God's Hands

There is so little any of us can do,
But I know that God will take care of you.
For He's so great and we're so small,
But He is mindful of us all
And I will say a little prayer
And "place you safely" in His care!

And so I commend you into God's Hands—
and there is no safer place in all the
universe in which to leave anyone,
than in the Hands of God.

And now, may He who lived in Galilee
And healed the many there
Be near to you and heal you, too,
And keep you in His care.

Faith for Dark Days

When "dark days" come,
    and they come to us all
We feel so helpless
    and lost and small
We cannot fathom
    the reason why
And it is futile
    for us to try
To find the answer,
    the reason or cause
For the master plan
    is without any flaws
And when the darkness
    shuts out the light
We must lean on faith
    to restore our sight
For there is nothing
    that we need to know
If we have faith
    that wherever we go
God will be there
    to help us bear
Our disappointments,
    pain and care
For He is our Shepherd
    our Father—our Guide
And you're never alone
    with the Lord at your side
So may the Great Physician
    attend you
And may His healing
    completely mend you.

Good Shepherd of the sheep,
you gather the lambs in your arms
and carry them in your bosom:
We commend to your loving care this child.
Relieve his pain, guard him from all danger,
restore to him your gifts of gladness and strength,
and raise him up to a life of service to you.
Hear us, we pray, for your dear Name's sake.
Amen.

The Paradox of Pain

Paradoxical though it is, there is nothing in life worthwhile that is not attained through suffering and conflict. But suffering and sorrow are not too great a price to pay for the enriching privilege of touching other lives with more compassion and deeper understanding. And all the sweetest things in life come to us on the "wings of pain and tears," giving us a new awareness of God's *greatness*, His *goodness*, and His *grace!*

I know for "certain-sure" that my trials and tribulations have transformed my life completely, and I am satisfied that my "afflictions" are truly "gifts sent in disguise," which sometimes we fail to recognize.

There Are Blessings in Everything

Blessings come in many guises
        That God alone in love devises,
And sickness which we dread so much
        Can bring a very "healing touch"—
For often on the "wings of pain"
        The peace we sought before in vain
Will come to us with "sweet surprise"
        For God is merciful and wise—
And through long hours of tribulation
        God gives us time for meditation,
And no sickness can be counted loss
        That teaches us to "bear our cross."

By your patience in suffering
you hallowed earthly pain
and gave us the example
of obedience to your Father's will:
Be near me in my time of weakness and pain;
sustain me by your grace,
that my strength and courage may not fail;
Heal me according to your will;
and help me always to believe
that what happens to me here
is of little account if you hold me in eternal life,
my Lord and my God.
Amen.

God's Tender Care

When trouble comes,
    as it does to us all
God is so great
    and we are so small—
But there is nothing
    that we need know
If we have faith
    that wherever we go
God will be waiting
    to help us bear
Our pain and sorrow,
    our suffering and care—
For no pain or suffering
    is ever too much
To yield itself
    to God's merciful touch!

A Time to Be Silent

Seek the LORD while he may be found;
    call on him while he is near
Let the wicked forsake his way
    and the evil man his thoughts.
Let him turn to the LORD,
    and he will have mercy on him,
    and to our God, for he will freely pardon.

"For my thoughts are not your thoughts,
    neither are your ways my ways,"
                    declares the LORD.
"As the heavens are higher than the earth,
    so are my ways higher than your ways
    and my thoughts than your thoughts.
As the rain and the snow
    come down from heaven,
and do not return to it

without watering the earth
and making it bud and flourish,
so that it yields seed for the sower and bread for
the eater,
so is my word that goes out from my mouth:
It will not return to me empty,
but will accomplish what I desire
and achieve the purpose for which I sent it.
You will go out in joy
and be led forth in peace;
the mountains and hills
will burst into song before you,
and all the trees of the field
will clap their hands."

Isaiah 55:6–12

A Prayer for Patience

God, teach me to be patient—
Teach me to go slow—
Teach me how to "wait on You"
When my way I do not know
Teach me sweet forbearance
When things do not go right
So I remain unruffled
When others grow uptight
Teach me how to quiet
My racing, rising heart

So I may hear the answer
You are trying to impart
Teach me to let go, dear God,
And pray undisturbed until
My heart is filled with inner peace
And I learn to know Your will!

O God of Peace
who has taught us that
in returning and rest we shall be saved,
in quietness and in confidence shall be our strength:
By the might of thy Spirit lift us,
we pray thee, to thy presence,
where we may be still and know that thou art God.
Amen.

The Peace of Meditation

So we may know God better
And feel His quiet power,
Let us daily keep in silence
A *meditation hour*—
For to understand God's greatness
And to use His gifts each day
The soul must learn to meet Him
In a meditative way.
For our Father tells His children
That if they would know His will
They must seek Him in the silence
When all is calm and still . . .
For nature's greatest forces
Are found in quiet things
Like softly falling snowflakes
Drifting down on angels' wings,
Or petals dropping soundlessly
From a lovely full-blown rose,
So God comes closest to us
When our souls are in repose . . .
So let us plan with prayerful care
To always allocate
A certain portion of each day
To be still and meditate . . .
For when everything is quiet
And we're lost in meditation,
Our soul is then preparing
For a deeper dedication
That will make it wholly possible
To quietly endure
The violent world around us—
For in God we are secure.

The Best Things

The best things are nearest:
breath in your nostrils,
light in your eyes,
flowers at your feet,
duties at your hand,
the path of Right just before you.

Then do not grasp at the stars,
but do life's plain, common work
as it comes, certain that
daily duties and daily bread
are the sweetest things of life.

Trouble

God help us to accept Your love
that You offer us so freely
And make us ever thankful
that You give it lavishly
But make us also conscious
that Your love comes in many ways
And not always just as happiness
and bright and shining days
But often You send trouble
and we foolishly reject it
Not realizing that it is Your Will
and we should joyously accept it
And in trouble and in gladness

we can always hear Your voice
If we listen in the silence
    and find a reason to rejoice.

Renewal

When life has lost its luster
    and it's filled with dull routine
When you long to run away from it
    seeking pastures "new and green"
Remember, no one runs away from life
    without finding when they do
You can't escape the thoughts you think
    that are pressing down on you
For though the scenery may be different
    it's the same old heart and mind
And the same old restless longings
    that you tried to leave behind
So when your heart is heavy
    and your day is dull with care
Instead of trying to escape
    why not withdraw in prayer
For in prayer there is renewal
    of the spirit, mind, and heart
For everything is lifted up
    in which God has a part. . . .
For when we go to God in prayer
    our thoughts are rearranged
So even though our problems
    have not been solved or changed
Somehow the good Lord gives us
    the power to understand
That He who holds tomorrow
    is the One who holds our hand.

This is another day, O Lord.
I know not what it will bring forth,
but make me ready, Lord,
for whatever it may be.
If I am to stand up, help me to stand bravely.
If I am to sit still, help me to sit quietly.
If I am to lie low, help me to do it patiently.
And if I am to do nothing, let me do it gallantly.
Amen.

The Voice of God

Within the crowded city . . . where life is swift and
　　fleet
Do you ever look for Jesus upon the busy street?
Above the noise and laughter that is empty, cruel, and
　　loud
Do you listen for the voice of God in the restless
　　surging crowd?
Do you pause in meditation upon life's thoroughfare
And offer up thanksgiving or say a word of prayer?
Well, if you would find the Saviour no need to search
　　afar
For God is all around you no matter where you are
And whether on a country road . . . or a busy crowded
　　street.

Seldom Seen

I don't see you as often as I used to, it's true
But that doesn't stop me from thinking of you.

And while life is crowded with things that annoy
And we seldom have time to see folks we enjoy

I want you to know you're too nice to forget
And I'll always be glad that you and I met

For you're that unforgettable kind
That stays mirrored in the heart and mind.

God Grant Me the Glory of "Thy Gift"

God, widen my vision so I may see
    the afflictions You have sent to me—
Not as a cross too heavy to bear
    that weighs me down in gloomy despair—
Not as somethng to hate and despise
    but a gift of love sent in disguise—
Something to draw me closer to You
    to teach me *patience* and *forbearance*, too—
Something to show me more clearly the way
    to serve You and love You more every day—
Something *priceless* and *precious* and *rare*
    that will keep me forever safe in Thy care
Aware of the spiritual strength that is mine
    if my selfish, small will is lost in Thine!

God Speaks

So when I looked at those flowers,
 I was looking at God
For they bloomed in His sun
 and grew in His sod
And each lovely flower
 was a "voice from above"
That whispered a message
 of Kindness and Love
For I feel in my heart,
 and I know you do, too,
That God speaks to us all
 through the kind things we do
And when I looked at those flowers
 I couldn't help but feel
That they brought heaven nearer
 and made God so real.

The words that make the soul
 rejoice
Are spoken by the heart's
 "still voice."

When the Pressures Mount

My days are so crowded
    and my hours are so few,
There's so little time
    and so much to do.

My work is unfinished
    and my desk is piled high,
And my unanswered mail
    seems to reach to the sky.
I'm pressured and pushed
    until I am "dizzy"
There's never a minute
    I'm not "crazily busy"
And sometimes, I wonder
    as I rush through the day
Does God really want me
    to hurry this way?
Why am I impatient
    and continually vexed,
And often bewildered,
    disturbed, and perplexed?
Perhaps, I'm too busy
    with my own selfish seeking
To hear the dear Lord
    when He's tenderly speaking.
I'm working so tensely
    in my self-centered way,
I've no time to listen
    for what God has to say
And hard as I work,
    at the end of the day
I know in my heart
    I did not "pay my way"

But God in His mercy
    looks down on us all
And though what we've done
    is so pitifully small
He makes us feel welcome
    to kneel down and pray
For the chance to do better
    as we start a new day!

The First Thing Every Morning and the Last Thing Every Night . . .

Were you too busy this morning
    to quietly stop and pray
Did you hurry and drink your coffee
    then frantically rush away?
consoling yourself by saying,
    "God will always be there
Waiting to hear my petitions
    ready to answer each prayer"
It's true the great generous Saviour
    forgives our transgressions each day
And patiently waits for "lost sheep"
    who constantly seem to stray—
But moments of prayer once omitted
    in the busy rush of the day
Can never again be recaptured
    for they silently slip away.
And we never get back the freshness
    that was wrapped in the morning prayer

That we were unable to offer
    because there was no time to spare
And no one regains that blessing
    that would have been theirs if they prayed
For blessings are lost forever
    in prayers that are often delayed
And strength is gained in the morning
    to endure the trials of the day
When we "visit with God in person"
    in a quiet and unhurried way.
For only through prayer that's unhurried
    can the needs of the day be met
And only in prayers said at evening
    can we sleep without fear or regret
For all of our errors and failures
    that we made in the course of the day
Are freely forgiven each nighttime
    when we kneel down and earnestly pray
For prayer is a time of refreshment
    which no one should ever omit
For our lives are strengthened and lengthened
    and made more useful by "it"
So seek the Lord in the morning
    and never forget Him at night
For prayer is an unfailing blessing
    that makes every burden seem light.

The Mystery of Prayer

Beyond that which words can interpret
Or theology can explain
The soul feels a "shower of refreshment"
That falls like the gentle rain
On hearts that are parched with problems
And are searching to find the way
To somehow attract God's attention
Through well-chosen words as they pray,
Not knowing that God in His wisdom
Can sense all man's worry and woe
For there is nothing man can conceal
That God does not already know
So kneel in prayer in His presence
And you'll find no need to speak
For softly in silent communion
God grants you the peace that you seek.

God, Are You There?

I'm way down here!
You're way up there!
Are You sure You can hear
My faint, faltering prayer?
For I'm so unsure
Of just how to pray—
To tell You the truth, God,
I don't know what to say.
I just know I am lonely
And vaguely disturbed,
Bewildered and restless,
Confused and perturbed . . .
And they tell me that prayer
Helps to quiet the mind
And to unburden the heart
For in stillness we find
A newborn assurance
That someone does care
And Someone does answer
Each small, sincere prayer!

Listen in the Quietness

To try to run away from life
    is impossible to do
For no matter where you chance to go
    your troubles follow you
For though the scenery's different
    when you look inside you'll find

The same deep restless longings
    that you thought you left behind.
So when life becomes a problem
    much too great for us to bear
Instead of trying to escape
    let us withdraw in prayer
For withdrawal means renewal
    if we withdraw to pray
And listen in the quietness
    to hear what God will say.

The LORD is my shepherd, I shall lack nothing.
    He makes me lie down in green pastures,
he leads me beside quiet waters,
    he restores my soul.
He guides me in paths of righteousness
    for his name's sake.
Even though I walk
    through the valley of the shadow of death,
I will fear no evil,
    for you are with me;
your rod and your staff,
    they comfort me.

You prepare a table before me
    in the presence of my enemies.
You anoint my head with oil;
    my cup overflows.
Surely goodness and love will follow me
    all the days of my life,
and I will dwell in the house of the LORD forever.

Psalm 23

Anywhere Is a Place of Prayer
if God Is There

I have prayed on my knees in the morning,
I have prayed as I walked along,
I have prayed in the silence and darkness
And I've prayed to the tune of a song—
I have prayed in the midst of triumph
And I've prayed when I suffered defeat,
I have prayed on the sands of the seashore
Where the waves of the ocean beat—
I have prayed in a velvet-hushed forest
Where the quietness calmed my fears,
I have prayed through suffering and heartache
When my eyes were blinded with tears—
I have prayed in churches and chapels,
Cathedrals and synagogues, too,
But often I've had the feeling
That my prayers were not getting through,
And I realized then that our Father
Is not really concerned where we pray
Or impressed by our manner of worship
Or the eloquent words we say . . .
He is only concerned with our feelings,
And He looks deep into our heart
And hears the "cry of our soul's deep need"
That no words could ever impart . . .
So it isn't the prayer that's expressive
Or offered in some special spot.
It's the sincere plea of a sinner
And God can tell whether or not
We honestly seek His forgiveness
And earnestly mean what we say,
And then and then only He answers
The prayer that we fervently pray.

An Unfailing Prescription

But my prescription for you right now is one that a noted preacher once recommended . . . and it never fails to work . . . if it is followed precisely and without fail.

When you awaken read the Twenty-third Psalm . . . do not recite it from memory . . . *read it very slowly* and *very carefully* and *with deep meditation.* Do this again after you have had breakfast and after lunch and then after dinner and just before you go to bed.

Do not read it hurriedly . . . but think about each word and phrase and let your mind soak up the wonderful assurance there is in these words. Most of us know this Psalm by heart but we repeat it without ever realizing the great and full meaning of it. It is the *most powerful piece of writing* in this world.

Just think what it means to know that the Lord is your Shepherd and that He is leading you and anointing your scars and "heart-hurt" with the balm of His love. The more you think about this the more you become aware of its power. You can heal your body and mind and heart with this Psalm. God promises to restore your soul, revive your weary body, take you into a cool, clear place where you can rest . . . and no matter how steep the hill or the mountain is, the Lord is going to climb it with you.

Just writing this has already given me strength. The sheep are never afraid because they know the Shepherd will lead them into green pastures beside the still waters . . . and so as you come to dark places in your life just reach out for the hand of the Shepherd. If you stop and get very quiet and still you feel *the presence of God.*

I often say this when I am troubled . . . and I imagine I am just a "little lamb" who doesn't know where to go and that I have no one to follow but the Shepherd.

But I know the Shepherd will not let me fall over the precipice and He will not let me drink in the swift water for I might slip and fall in and I know that no matter what happens He will go with me even through the valley of the shadows. And with that knowledge *what is there to fear?*

He will bring you safely through no matter which "side of life or death" is your destination. *You cannot lose . . .* for *He brings his children safely through everything.*

Now, my dear, you just do this every day for a few weeks and you will be surprised *how calm and wonderful you feel.*

A Time to Mourn

As the deer pants for streams of water,
*   so my soul pants for you, O God.*
My soul thirsts for God, for the living God.
*   When can I go and meet with God?*
My tears have been my
*   food day and night,*
while men say to me all day long,
*   'Where is your God?"*
These things I remember
*   as I pour out my soul:*
how I used to go with the multitude,
*   leading the procession to the house of God,*
with shouts of joy and thanksgiving
*   among the festive throng.*

Why are you downcast, O my soul?
*   Why so disturbed within me?*
Put your hope in God,
*   for I will yet praise him,*
*   my Savior and my God.*

My soul is downcast within me;
*   therefore I will remember you*

from the land of the Jordan,
*   the heights of Hermon—from Mount Mizar.*
Deep calls to deep
*   in the roar of your waterfalls;*
all your waves and breakers
*   have swept over me.*

By day the LORD directs his love,
*   at night his song is with me—*
*   a prayer to the God of my life.*

I say to God my Rock,
*   "Why have you forgotten me?*
Why must I go about mourning,
*   oppressed by the enemy?"*

My bones suffer mortal agony
*   as my foes taunt me,*
saying to me all day long,
*   'Where is your God?"*

Why are you downcast, O my soul?
*   Why so disturbed within me?*
Put your hope in God,
*   for I will yet praise him,*
*   my Savior and my God.*

Psalm 42

The Bright Side

I'm looking out the window
        and the day is drab and dreary,
And I'm trying to console myself
        by thinking something cheery

I know it's simply horrible
        to get in such a slump
And I also know it's up to me
        to get across this hump
And I realize I'm selfish
        to mention this to you
For, gee, you might be feeling
        a little "low-down," too
But often when I feel like this
        I tell myself it's true
That I am not the only one
        who feels "low-down and blue"
And just knowing there are others
        who feel the way I do
Renews my sinking spirit
        and keeps me smiling through
And knowing that it's natural
        to take a "spirit-dive"
Provides the spunk and courage
        to hang on and survive
And while there are a lot of moods
        that we can drive away
By looking on the bright side
        in all we do and say,
There also is a loneliness
        that God meant us to feel
But, gee, it sure is mighty hard
        to know which one is real
And I'd hate to be a "sad sack"
        who never saw the sun
And just complained that every day
        was such a dreary one
But I know that all the dark days
        are just part of God's plan
We should accept them graciously
        and do the best we can . . .

So I'll just keep on trying
　　for I know it's "Gospel true"
There never was a cloud so dark
　　the sun could not shine through!

I know, dear, this will be a period of physical pain and "heart-hurt" for you all, but it will also be a deep spiritual experience. It is terrible, but it is wonderful, too. Only through great suffering can we really come to know what God is really like, and inner strength comes from facing trouble and suffering and enduring it.

God wants us to "reap a great spiritual crop" from "the seeds of suffering and sorrow." And remember, God never makes mistakes and He never "plows" where He does not intend to "sow seeds" . . . and when He "sows spiritual seeds," there is always a "crop" to fill "the storehouse of the soul" to overflowing!

There are days so dark that I search in vain for the hand of my Friend Divine.

The End of the Road Is But a Bend in the Road

When we feel we have nothing left to give
　　and we are sure that the "song has ended"—
When our day seems over and the shadows fall
　　and the darkness of night has descended.

Where can we go to find the strength
        to valiantly keep on trying,
Where can we find the hand that will dry
        the tears that the heart is crying—
There's but one place to go and that is to God
        and, dropping all pretense and pride,
We can pour out our problems without restraint
        and gain strength with Him at our side—
And together we stand at life's crossroads
        and view what we think is the end,
But God has a much bigger vision
        and He tells us it's only a bend—
For the road goes on and is smoother,
        and the "pause in the song" is a "rest,"
And the part that's unsung and unfinished
        is the sweetest and richest and best—
So rest and relax and grow stronger,
        let go and let God share your load,
Your work is not finished or ended,
        you've just come to "a bend in the road."

The Seasons of the Soul

Why am I cast down
        and despondently sad
When I long to be happy
        and joyous and glad?
Why is my heart heavy
        with unfathomable weight
As I try to escape
        this soul-saddened state?

I ask myself often—
      "What makes life this way,
Why is the song silenced
      in the heart that was gay?"
And then with God's help
      it all becomes clear,
The *Soul* has its *Seasons*
      just the same as the year—
I, too, must pass through
      life's autumn of dying,
A desolate period
      of "heart-hurt" and crying,
Followed by winter
      in whose frostbitten hand
My heart is as frozen
      as the snow-covered land—
Yes, man, too, must pass
      through the seasons God sends,
Content in the knowledge
      that everything ends,
And, oh, what a blessing
      to know there are reasons
And to find that our soul
      must, too, have its seasons—
Bounteous Seasons
      and *Barren Ones*, too,
Times for rejoicing
      and times to be blue,
But meeting these seasons
      of dark desolation
With strength that is born
      of anticipation
That comes from knowing
      that "autumn-time sadness"
Will surely be followed
      by a "springtime of gladness."

Dark Shadows Fall in the Lives of Us All

Sickness and sorrow
    come to us all,
But through it we grow
    and learn to "stand tall"—
For trouble is "part
    and parcel of life"
And no man can grow
    without struggle and strife,
And the more we endure
    with patience and grace
The stronger we grow
    and the more we can face—
And the more we can face,
    the greater our love,
And with love in our hearts
    we are more conscious of
The pain and the sorrow
    in lives everywhere,
So it is through trouble
    that we learn how to share.

In Hours of Discouragement
God Is Our Encouragement

Sometimes we feel uncertain
And unsure of everything,
Afraid to make decisions,
Dreading what the day will bring—
We keep wishing it were possible
To dispel all fear and doubt
And to understand more readily
Just what life is all about—
God has given us the answers
Which too often go unheeded,
But if we search His promises
We'll find everything that's needed
To lift our faltering spirits
And renew our courage, too,
For there's absolutely nothing
Too much for God to do—
For the Lord is our salvation
And our strength in every fight,
Our redeemer and protector,
Our eternal guiding light—
He has promised to sustain us,
He's our refuge from all harms,
And underneath this refuge,
Are the everlasting arms—
So cast your burden on Him,
Seek His counsel when distressed,
And go to Him for comfort
When you're lonely and oppressed—
For God is our encouragement
In trouble and in trials,
And in suffering and in sorrow
He will turn our tears to smiles.

Blessings Come in Many Guises

When troubles come
    and things go wrong,
And days are cheerless
    and nights are long,
We find it so easy
    to give in to despair
By magnifying
    the burdens we bear—
We add to our worries
    by refusing to try
To look for "the rainbow"
    in an overcast sky—
And the blessing God sent
    in a "darkened disguise"
Our troubled hearts
    fail to recognize,
Not knowing God sent it
    not to distress us
But to strengthen our faith
    and redeem us and bless us.

"Do not let your hearts be troubled. Trust in God; trust also in me. In my Father's house are many rooms; if it were not so, I would have told you. I am going there to prepare a place for you. And if I go and prepare a place for you, I will come back and take you to be with me that you also may be where I am. You know the way to the place where I am going.

"Peace I leave with you; my peace I give you. I do not give to you as the world gives. Do not let your hearts be troubled and do not be afraid.

"You heard me say, 'I am going away and I am coming back to you.' If you loved me, you would be glad that I am going to the Father, for the Father is greater than I. I have told you now before it happens, so that when it does happen you will believe."

John 14:1–4; 27–29

A Bright New World

We feel so sad when those we love
Are touched by death's dark hand,
But it would ease our sorrow
If we could but understand
That death is just a gateway
That all men must pass through
And on the other side of death,
In a world that's bright and new,
Our loved ones wait to welcome us
To that land free from all tears
Where joy becomes eternal
And time is not counted by years.

When I Must Leave You

When I must leave you
    for a little while,
Please do not grieve
    and shed wild tears
And hug your sorrow
    to you through the years,
But start out bravely
    with a gallant smile;
And for my sake
    and in my name
Live on and do
    all things the same,
Feed not your loneliness
    on empty days,
But fill each waking hour
    in useful ways,
Reach out your hand
    in comfort and in cheer
And I in turn will comfort you
    and hold you near;
And never, never
    be afraid to die,
For I am waiting
    for you in the sky!

On the Loss of a Child

There are some things that no words have ever been invented to fit . . . and there is so little I can say to soften your sorrow or lessen the stabbing pain that fills your hearts today for your loss is so keen and so new and so deep that your days are made up of nothing but "lost-loneliness" and "heart-hurt" at present, but in the months ahead you will gain strength that will enable you to realize that life stretches into *eternity* and it never ends, and your little one is not dead, she has only gone "back home to God," and she is hopping along gaily on the tip of a fluffy cloud and scampering through fields of enjoyment with the wind in her hair and blowing bubbles out of moonbeams and playing hide-and-seek with the stars.

This deep emotional and spiritual experience that you are sharing is one that will link you even closer together as you go through the years . . . for to share happiness brings joy to the heart—but to share sorrow is treasure for the soul, for love is a unity of the soul, and sorrow is only a closer joining. And in this tragedy you were drawn a little closer to God and to one another. And while your hearts hurt you now, you will find a newer and deeper beauty of "togetherness" since this tragedy came to clear your vision. Life takes on a deeper meaning and significance with every spiritual experience that is shared, and this truly is another evidence of the mystery of life and the impenetrable greatness of the Master Builder whose plans for our lives are without flaws, for He sees beyond the horizon of Today into the Eternal Tomorrow. We are all a part of God, and God is everywhere, and your little one just decided to go back to heaven instead of continuing her journey in a world so full of restlessness and turmoil. God is at the beginning and the end of everything, and there is nothing beyond Him . . . so find comfort in that thought.

Home at Last

There are no words, what can I say
    At last her sweet soul winged its way
To peace and freedom in the sky
    Where never again will she suffer or cry
It's all a part of God's Great Plan . . .
    Which is a mystery to man
We cannot understand His ways
    Nor can we count our earthly days
But who are we to question and doubt
    God knoweth well what He's about
He knew she longed to "go to sleep"
    Where only angels a vigil keep
The pain of living grew too great
    No longer could she stay and wait
She did not want to leave you, dear
    But she had finished her work down here
So she closed her eyes and when she awoke
    These are the words the Master spoke,
Welcome, dear child, you are Home at last
    And now the burden of living is past
There's work for you in My Kingdom, dear
    And you are needed and wanted here."
So weep not, she's just gone on ahead
    Don't think of her as being dead.
She's out of sight for a little while
    And you'll miss her touch, and her little smile
But you know she is safe in the home above
    Where there is nothing but Peace and Love
And, surely, you would not deny her peace
    And you're glad she has found release
Think of her there as a soul that is free.
    And Home at last, where she wanted to be.

On the Other Side of Death

Death is a Gateway
    we all must pass through
To reach that Fair Land
    where the soul's born anew,
For man's born to die
    and his sojourn on earth
Is a short span of years
    beginning with birth
And like pilgrims we wander
    until death takes our hand
And we start on our journey
    to God's Promised Land,
A place where we'll find
    no suffering nor tears,
Where Time is not counted
    by days, months, or years
And in this Fair City
    that God has prepared
Are unending joys
    to be happily shared
With all of our loved ones
    who patiently wait
On Death's Other Side
    to open "the Gate"!

Somewhere there is a Life Eternal
Somewhere there is a Home, above.
There is no night without a dawning,
Beyond this death is God and Love.

O merciful Father,
who hast taught us in thy holy Word
that thou dost not willingly
afflict or grieve the children of men:
Look with pity upon the sorrows of thy servant
for whom our prayers are offered.
Remember him, O Lord, in mercy,
nourish his soul with patience,
comfort him with a sense of thy goodness,
lift up they countenance upon him,
and give him peace.
Amen.

Waiting at Eternity's Door

Death beckoned him
    with outstretched hand
And whispered softly
    of "an unknown land" . . .
But he was not
    afraid to go
For though the path
    he did not know,
He took death's hand
    without a fear
For God who safely
    brought him here
Had promised He
    would lead the way
Into eternity's
    bright day . . .
For none of us
    need go alone
Into the valley

that's unknown
But guided by
    our Father's hand
We journey to
    the Promised Land . . .
And as his loving,
    faithful wife
Who shared his home
    and heart and life,
You will find comfort
    for your grief,
In knowing death
    brought sweet relief,
For now he is free
    from all suffering and pain
And your "great loss"
    became his gain . . .
You know his love
    is with you still,
For he loved you in life
    and he always will . . .
For love like yours
    can never end
Because it is
    the perfect blend
Of joys and sorrows,
    smiles and tears
That just grows stronger
    with the years
And love like this
    can never die,
For you "take it with you
    to the sky" . . .
So think of your loved one
    as living above
No farther away

than your undying love . . .
And now he is happy and free
        once more
And he waits for you
        at eternity's door.

I love the LORD, for he heard my voice;
        he heard my cry for mercy.
Because he turned his ear to me,
        I will call on him as long as I live.

The cords of death entangled me,
        the anguish of the grave came upon me;
        I was overcome by trouble and sorrow.
Then I called on the name of the LORD:
        "O LORD, save me!"

The LORD is gracious and righteous;
        our God is full of compassion.
The LORD protects the simplehearted;
        when I was in great need, he saved me.

Be at rest once more, O my soul,
        for the LORD has been good to you.

I just want to say again that, if we never suffered tragedy and we never felt sorrow, how could our souls ever grow? In my husband's tragic death, which was so hurried and unscheduled, it was difficult for me, when I was very young, to see what the purpose could have been. But now I know that he sacrificed his life that my life might be lived in a fuller and richer way, for his sudden death transformed my entire life. I never could have done what I am doing now if I had not felt the pangs of sorrow, for you cannot dry the tears of those who weep unless you have cried yourself.

I know, when death comes flashing out of a bright sky, suddenly and unexpectedly in the midst of youthful enjoyment when life is flushed with hope and filled with dreams, it is very, very difficult to accept God's judgment. It is hard to reconcile ourselves to such a loss when God asks us to give up someone young and in mid-career with abundant years stretching ahead of them, for to have a life so suddenly silenced is beyond our understanding.

But there is something brave and beautiful in passing at this "high peak" while standing on "tiptoe" into new fields of usefulness. And you must realize, dear, that he just rose unencumbered to meet God and he is safe and free, where all the problems of this restless, violent world will no longer disturb his young mind.

May God comfort you and show you the way. But remember, God does not comfort us to make us more comfortable. He comforts us so that *we may also become comforters.*

Words say so little when hearts mean so much.

Death Opens the Door to Life Evermore

We live a short while on earth below,
Reluctant to die for we do not know
Just what "dark death" is all about
And so we view it with fear and doubt,
Not certain of what is around the bend
We look on death as the final end
To all that made us a mortal being
And yet there lies just beyond our seeing
A beautiful life so full and complete
That we should leave with hurrying feet
To walk with God by sacred streams
Amid beauty and peace beyond our dreams—
For all who believe in the risen Lord
Have been assured of this reward,
And death for them is just "graduation"
To a higher realm of wide elevation—
For life on earth is a transient affair,
Just a few brief years in which to prepare
For a life that is free from pain and tears
Where time is not counted by hours or years—
For death is only the method God chose
To colonize heaven with the souls of those
Who by their apprenticeship on earth
Proved worthy to dwell in the land of new birth—
So death is not sad . . . it's a time for elation,
A joyous transition . . . the soul's emigration
Into a place where the soul's safe and free
To live with God through eternity!

For you, O LORD, have delivered my soul from death,
*   my eyes from tears,*
*   my feet from stumbling,*
that I may walk before the LORD
*   in the land of the living.*
I believed; therefore I said,
*   "I am greatly afflicted."*
And in my dismay I said,
*   "All men are liars."*
How can I repay the LORD
*   for all his goodness to me?*
I will lift up the cup of salvation
*   and call on the name of the LORD.*
I will fulfill my vows to the LORD
*   in the presence of all his people.*

Precious in the sight of the LORD
*   is the death of his saints.*

Psalms 116:1–15

A Time for Peace

Rejoice in the Lord always. I will say it again: Rejoice! Let your gentleness be evident to all. The Lord is near. Do not be anxious about anything, but in everything, by prayer and petition, with thanksgiving, present your requests to God. And the peace of God, which transcends all understanding, will guard your hearts and your minds in Christ Jesus.

Finally, brothers, whatever is true, whatever is noble, whatever is right, whatever is pure, whatever is lovely, whatever is admirable—if anything is excellent or praiseworthy—think about such things. Whatever you have learned or received or heard from me, or seen in me—put it into practice. And the God of peace will be with you.

Philippians 4:4–9

There is no prayer
too great or small
To ask of God
who hears them all—
So put your problems
in God's Hand
And do not ask
to understand!

A Little Closer to God

These past few months I have been going through
many hours of "soul searching" and walking
through "dark hours" that come to us all. But
I know God is behind the "dark cloud" that
engulfs me, and I must endure it until He
removes the "darkness," for this is not a
destructive experience but a constructive one.
I am sure He is trying to awaken me to a new
awareness of how to best serve Him. And after
my old self dies completely, I will have moved
a little closer to God!

Days of Beauty and Peace

For God in His loving and all-wise way
Makes the heart that once was young and gay
Serene and more gentle and less restless, too,
Content to remember the joys it once knew
And all that I sought on the pathway of pleasure
Becomes but a memory to cherish and treasure—
The fast pace grows slower and the spirit serene,
And the soul can envision what the eyes have not
    seen
And so while life's springtime is sweet to recall,
The autumn of life is the best time of all,
For our wild, youthful yearnings all gradually cease
And God fills our days with *beauty* and *peace!*

I lift up my eyes to the hills—
    where does my help come from?
My help comes from the LORD,
    the Maker of heaven and earth.

He will not let your foot slip—
    he who watches over you will not slumber;
Indeed, he who watches over Israel
    will neither slumber nor sleep.

The LORD watches over you—
    the LORD is your shade at your right hand;
the sun will not harm you by day,
    nor the moon by night.

The LORD will keep you from all harm—
    he will watch over your life;
the LORD will watch over your coming and going
    both now and forevermore.

Psalm 121

The Peace You Seek

Another hill and sometimes a mountain
But just when you reach the peak—
Your weariness is lifted
And you find the peace you seek

I Said a Little Prayer for You

I said a little prayer for you
        and I asked the Lord above
To keep you safely in His care
        and enfold you in His love
I did not ask for fortune
        for riches or for fame
I only asked for blessings
        in the Saviour's Holy name
Blessings to surround you
        in times of trial and stress
And inner joy to fill your heart
        with peace and happiness.

God Is Always Beside You

Whatever betide you,
        God is always beside you—
So "let not your heart be troubled"
        nor your mind be filled with fear
For you have God's reassurance
        that He's always very near,
And no prayer goes unanswered
        and no one walks alone
And if we trust the Saviour
        we are never on our own—
And the "helping hands of Anniston"

will be praying for you, too,
And in the loving Father's care
things will all be well for you.

Priceless Treasures

What could I give you that would truly please
In "topsy-turvy times" like these?
I can't give you freedom from vexations
Or even lessen your irritations
I can't take away or even make less
The things that annoy, disturb, and distress
For stores don't sell a single thing
To make the heart that's troubled sing
They sell "the new look" suave and bland
But nothing that lends a "helping hand,"
They sell rare gifts that are ultra-smart
But nothing to warm or comfort the heart
The joys of life that cheer and bless,
The stores don't sell, I must confess
But friends and prayers are "priceless treasures"
Beyond all monetary measures . . .

And so I say a special prayer
        that God will keep you in His care . . .
And if I can ever help you, dear,
        in any way throughout the year,
You've only to call, for as long as I live
        "Such as I have, I freely give!"

Therefore I tell you, do not worry about your life, what you will eat or drink; or about your body, what you will wear. Is not life more important than food, and the body more important than clothes? Look at the birds of the air; they do not sow or reap or store away in barns, and yet your heavenly Father feeds them. Are you not much more valuable than they? Who of you by worrying can add a single hour to his life?

"And why do you worry about clothes? See how the lilies of the field grow. They do not labor or spin. Yet I tell you that not even Solomon in all his splendor was dressed like one of these. If that is how God clothes the grass of the field, which is here today and tomorrow is thrown into the fire, will he not much more clothe you, O you of little faith? So do not worry, saying, 'What shall we eat?' or 'What shall we drink?' or 'What shall we wear?' For the pagans run after all these things, and your heavenly Father knows that you need them. But seek first his kingdom and his righteousness, and all these things will be given to you as well. Therefore do not worry about tomorrow, for tomorrow will worry about itself. Each day has enough trouble of its own."

Matthew 6:25–34

The Way to Love and Peace

There is no thinking person
Who can stand untouched today
And view the world around us
Slowly drifting to decay
Without feeling deep within them
A silent, unnamed dread
As they contemplate the future
That lies frighteningly ahead
And as the "clouds of chaos"
Gather in man's muddled mind,
And he searches for the answer
He *alone* can never find,
Let us recognize we're facing
Problems man has never solved,
And with all our daily efforts
Life grows more and more involved,
But our future will seem brighter
And we'll meet with less resistance
If we call upon our Father
And seek Divine Assistance
For the spirit can unravel
Many tangled, knotted threads
That defy the skill and power
Of the world's best hands and heads,
And our plans for growth and progress,
Of which we all have dreamed,
Cannot survive materially
Unless our spirits are redeemed
For only when the mind of man
Is united with the soul
Can Love and Peace combine to make
Our lives complete and whole.

Tender Watch

When the way seems long
  and the Day is dark,
And we can't hear the song
  of the thrush or the lark,
And our hearts are heavy
  with sickness and care,
And we are lost in the
  depths of despair . . .
That is the time
  when faith alone
Can lead us out of
  "the dark unknown,"
For faith to believe
  when "the way is rough"
And faith to "hang on"
  when "the going is tough"
Will never fail to
  pull us through
And bring us Strength
  and Comfort, too . . .
For it's not ours
  to question "why,"
For only "our Father"
  who dwells on high
Knows all the answers
  and reasons, too,
And His master plan
  is Perfect and True . . .
So do not try to
  understand,
Just take the Saviour's
  loving hand

And let Him lead you
    where He will
Through "Pastures green"
    and "Waters still" . . .
And though the way
    ahead seems steep,
Be not afraid
    for He will keep
Tender watch
    through night and day
And He will hear
    each prayer you pray . . .
So place yourself
    in His loving care
And He will gladly
    help you bear
Whatever lies ahead
    of you
For God will see you
    safely through!

Grant, O God,
that your holy and life-giving Spirit
may move every human heart
that barriers which divide us may crumble,
suspicions disappear, and hatreds cease;
that our divisions being healed,
we may live in justice and peace.
Amen.

Let Not Your Heart Be Troubled

Whenever I am troubled
    and lost in deep despair
I bundle all my troubles up
    and go to God in prayer
I tell Him I am heartsick
    and lost and lonely, too,
That my mind is deeply burdened
    and I don't know what to do
But I know He stilled the tempest
    and calmed the angry sea
And I humbly ask if in His love
    He'll do the same for me
And then I just keep quiet
    and think only thoughts of Peace
And if I abide in stillness
    my "restless murmurings" cease.

Peace Begins in the Home and the Heart

Peace is not something you fight for
With bombs and missiles that kill,
Nor can it be won in a "battle of words"
Man fashions by scheming and skill
For men who are greedy and warlike,
Whose avarice for power cannot cease,
Can never contribute in helping
To bring this world nearer to peace
For in seeking peace for all people
There is only one place to begin
And that is in each home and heart—
For the fortress of peace is within!

"Come to me, all you who are weary and burdened, and I will give you rest. Take my yoke upon you and learn from me, for I am gentle and humble in heart, and you will find rest for your souls. For my yoke is easy and my burden is light."

Matthew 11:28–30

No Favor Do I Seek Today

I come not to ask, to plead or implore You,
I just come to tell You how much I adore You,
For to kneel in Your Presence makes me feel blest
For I know that You know all my needs best . . .
And it fills me with joy just to linger with You
As my soul You replenish and my heart You renew
For prayer is much more than just asking for things—
It's the Peace and Contentment that Quietness brings . . .
So thank You again for Your Mercy and Love
And for making me heir to Your Kingdom above!